Intuition

Your Most Powerful Tool

by LINDA JOHNSON

ANGELICO BOOKS

TABLE OF CONTENTS

INTRODUCTION

Gut feeling. Hunch. Odd Feeling. Whatever name we give it, we get messages from our intuition every day. What if one could learn to understand these messages and use them to improve one's life?

When you are truly in communication with your intuition, your life can become easier, even effortless. Amazing synchronicities, creative insights, and a certainty and knowing that maybe you've only felt for brief moments become a part of your daily existence.

On a practical level, honing your intuition will help you make better decisions more easily, trust your own senses, and feel more connected and in the flow.

Maybe you've already explored your intuition and have felt frustrated with getting different results on different days. Maybe you've picked up other intuition books and found them full of mystical mayhem. Maybe this is your first adventure into the world of intuition. Maybe you just bought this book on a hunch that this is the time for you to learn to use your intuition to live a happier, more complete, life.

Well, you are in the right place.

This book will help you to identify how your intuition communicates with you, and provide you with a program to learn to listen to your intuition more easily and integrate these messages into your life.

I've also included access to two free audio files that will guide you in exploring your intuition and making decisions using your intuition. I include links to them later in the book.

Your intuition has been residing inside of you all along, patiently waiting to be called into action. If you haven't experienced it lately, you can easily coax it out of its hiding place. You can develop this innate ability we were all born with.

We'll start by dispelling some myths about intuition, discuss the different types of intuition. Then we'll get into specific methods you can use to receive clear messages from your intuition.

Debunking common intuition myths

The concept of intuition is difficult for the rational mind to grasp. After all, your intuition doesn't try to explain things; it just tells you what to do. In a society where constantly asking why, questioning the credibility of a source and challenging authority are staples in information gathering (at least that's what's revered in the fields of law, scientific research and journalism), it is easy for the mind to create myths to fill in the gaps of its understanding about intuition.

Myth # 1: Intuition and logic don't go together. Different people have different thoughts on what acceptable modes of thinking are and what are unacceptable. While intuitive people tend to trust in the knowing from within, logical and scientific-minded people need physical evidence to believe in things. If walking on hot coals is more reasonable than listening to an unexplainable voice, the biggest of skeptics will walk on hot coals first. However, the greatest minds in the science community are not always the greatest skeptics. In fact, these are the people who openly acknowledged and used their own intuition to make breakthrough discoveries that a lot of us take for granted today. No less than Albert Einstein himself said, "The intuitive mind is a sacred gift and the rational mind is a faithful servant. We have created a society that honors the servant and has forgotten the gift." Does this mean the rational mind is a slave to the intuitive mind? Of course not! The intuitive and logical sides of your mind are two-and-two. Your intuition "tells" you things you can't seem to get out of your mind and so your logical mind moves to investigate why this is so.

Myth # 2: Intuition is simply 'women's intuition'. There may be some slight bit of truth to this myth, but even this small inkling of truth has been so manipulated by the rational mind. Research shows that women generally have a thicker corpus callosum, that thick strip of nerves between the right brain and the left brain that connects both hemispheres. This means women are more likely to relate their intuitive experiences with their everyday logical, rational thoughts more easily than men can. So that's why men can't seem to lie successfully to women – women really are better at picking up the little details! But only slightly better. That women have thicker corpus callosums does not imply that men are less intuitive. In fact, while women have better-connected brain hemispheres in general, there are more instances of men having unusually larger corpus callosums. Case in point, Albert Einstein.

Myth # 3: You can't access intuition on your own. The thing is people cannot force their intuitive thoughts to pop into view, but they can set up all the right conditions for intuition to happen. Intuition can be a blinding flash of inspiration or a sudden knowing without knowing why, but intuition isn't always that spontaneous. It comes easily when the mind is ready and you deliberately welcome the power of intuition into your life. The rest of this book is dedicated to developing your intuition in different ways so you can have easy access to it.

Myth # 4: Intuitive people are born, not made. There are people who were fortunate enough to be born with the ability to listen to their intuition without trying. And then there are people, perhaps people like you who are reading this book, for whom intuition is a gift that has to be honed. The mind is a very powerful thing, yet we don't often remember that we are more powerful than our minds. Your brain is an adaptable organ that can easily change and adjust to new learning over time. Thorough practice can help your mind develop the ability to send you intuitive experiences on a more regular basis.

Myth # 5: Being intuitive and psychic are the same thing. Some people may see it this way, but there is absolutely zero prerequisite to be able to step into the world of spirits if you want to access your intuition.

Myth # 6: There are no practical uses for intuition. On the contrary, our intuition plays a role in practically every aspect of our daily lives. Didn't you have that feeling of everything being right when you purchased your new house with your husband? Or when you made a major business decision that was going to determine whether you got the deal or not? How about when you sensed the tension in your best friend's relationship and decided to have a heart-to-heart talk with her and she can spilled the beans so you were able to help her deal with it? Or when you attended a seminar and suddenly smiled at a stranger because you felt like he was going to be helpful in your business? Whether you like it or not, your intuition is present throughout your daily life.

Access Meditations and Other Resources at this website: http://www.AngelicoBooks.com/Intuition

UNDERSTANDING INTUITION

What is intuition? Researchers now believe that two forms of intuition are available to us. I call them 'intuition from experience' and 'intuition from the field'. Often it's difficult to tell which one you're tapping. Their characteristics tend to overlap and the result is the same: a decision made that transcends all the quantifiable evidence with which you're presented. So what's the difference?

Intuition from experience

Also known as 'intuition-as-expertise,' because of the way in which you acquire this information. This is the intuition you get from being an expert in something from experiencing it over and over and drawing conclusions.

In some cases you utilize this inner sense based on what you've learned from your experiences. You draw upon the outcomes of similar circumstances and compare them to the decision at hand. In a way, you're playing the odds. You know that the last time you were presented with a similar situation A plus B equaled C.

So you choose that equation to use.This may go against the grain of some individuals who are advising you to use the equation that A plus B equals D. But they aren't drawing from the same pool of experience you are. Your decision to them may appear to be intuitive thinking. And in many ways it is.

But it's also clearly calling upon your prior resources. These resources are those you explicitly learned as well as those you acquired implicitly, without realizing it, through your powers of observation. The observational powers of your subconscious mind to collect, save and file fragments of information is amazing. It's this 'secret' information that your subconscious has but doesn't share with you that makes this process so astounding to so many of us.

In his book, *The Biology of Belief*, Dr. Bruce Lipton discusses how the conscious mind can only process about 40 pieces of information a second, while the subconscious mind can process over 40,000 pieces of information per second. It's like 1000 movies are going on all around you that your subconscious mind can watch, but your conscious mind can only watch one. Imagine what it will be like when you learn to communicate with your subconscious and access all that information!

One of the most prominent experiments on how the subconscious mind sends you signals was conducted by scientists at the University of Iowa. The scientists ask people to play a game with four decks of cards. For each round, the player was asked to draw a card from one of the decks. The winner depends on the value of the card he draws. Of course, the decks were rigged. Two of them all had winning cards of high value while the other two were completely stacked with losers. By the time the players reached 10 rounds, the subconscious mind already knew the scientists' bluff. In fact, it was trying to call the player out on it by ringing all the stress bells sweating palms, faster heartbeats, slower digestion rates, the works!

But most of the players didn't become conscious of the setup until 80 rounds. "If you find yourself in a situation that's making you feel nervous, you may have spotted a reason for concern without even knowing it," says Joy Hirsh, Ph.D., director of the MRI Research Center at the Columbia University Medical Center. "Pay attention to the sensation."

Intuition from the Field

If you've watched the movie, *The Secret*, you may be familiar with this type of Intuition. It is the ability to draw information out of the 'collective unconscious', or through the 'field'. The growing research and relation between this type of Intuition and quantum physics is beyond the scope of this book.

Access Meditations and Other Resources at this website: http://www.AngelicoBooks.com/Intuition

LEARNING HOW INTUITION COMMUNICATES WITH YOU

Each of us receives information in different ways. Some people learn better through reading, while others prefer watching a demonstrative video. Some simply put on a pair of headphones, close their eyes and listen. Just like with the regular senses, we all have different preferences in the use of our intuitive senses. Yes, we do have them. Where do you suppose we get all that information from if there are no channels for us to receive them?

I like to refer to them as the 'five sisters'. All of them have the same name, Clair. They are: Clairvoyance for sight, Clairaudience for hearing, Clairalience for smell, Clairsentience for feeling and Claircognizance for simply knowing. A person may be predisposed to one or two of these senses, but it is possible to combine your skills in each of them once you become really familiar with how to use your dominant sensing abilities.

The presence of the intuitive senses is not merely attributed to theory. Psychologists studying the phenomenon of blindsight attest to the fact that we receive information that bypasses the regular senses and veers straight towards the subconscious. Neuroscientist and blindsight researcher, Beatrice de Gelder, Ph.D., explains, "We all process things that we're not consciously aware of – it's a feeling of knowing that uses an older brain structure."

Blindsight occurs when people who were rendered blind after an accident are still able to 'see' the things in front of them, despite not having the physical faculty to do so. For example, a blind person with blindsight can find his way through a maze without the use of his hands for feeling his way through. Or he can still name the emotion registered on another person's face despite the lack of vision. Of course, not very many people experience blindsight, but it clearly illustrates how information passes through the unknowing filters of the conscious mind.

Let's take a closer look at each of the Clair sisters.

Clairvoyance

When you can clearly see things with your mind's eye, you are most likely a clairvoyant. Intuition comes to you in snapshots or moving images inside your head and often appears in the form of visions, dreams, fuzzy daydreams or just sudden pictures that pop into your head. These may be in black-and-white or in full color. It doesn't matter because the images that clairvoyants see are powerful images that contain meaningful symbols.

Signs you're a clairvoyant:

- You have very vivid and memorable dreams.

- You can easily picture an apple inside your head, turn it around and view it with your mind's eye from all angles.

- You notice things moving from the corner of your eye.

- You come up with visual solutions to your problems.

- You have a clear image of what you want things to look like, such as when planning an event or designing a mural.

Clairaudience

That tiny voice inside your head may indicate more than a mental disorder after all. You might be clairaudient, or able to clearly hear information on a different level. It may sound like your own voice speaking to you or it may be a completely different voice. You can distinguish this intuitive voice from the rattle of your own conscious thought when it gives you a feeling of peace from within rather than the usual anxiousness that you get from talking to yourself too much. Clairaudient people don't only hear voices. Sometimes, they also hear songs, music or a ringing inside their heads.

Signs you're a clairaudient:

- You have heard a clear and persistent voice speak directly to you and you know it wasn't you.

- You hear voices or music during the first moments of waking up.

- You talk to yourself a lot (and listen).

- You hear things outside of your head but you look around and you find that nothing is there.

Clairalience

The ability to smell odors when they are not there is sometimes associated with detecting the presence of deceased loved ones, but it can also mean it is just your intuition working through your intuitive 'nose'. You can smell different things like perfume, spicy food, cigarette smoke, flowers or burning food.

Signs you're a clairalient:

- You smell distinctive smells without a physical source.

- You smell things and this gives you information. For example, a friend of mine who is a cook can tell when food in the oven is done, even if she didn't put it into the oven. She can walk into a house where food is cooking and tell the exact moment it should come out of the oven.

Clairsentience

This is what you are tapping into when you say you have a 'gut feeling' about something. Clairsentience, or clearly feeling, involves the different sensations your body can experience. It is that sinking feeling in your stomach, the shivers down your spine and the hairs on your arms standing on end. It is also that headache you get from out of nowhere, the extreme emotions you suddenly feel and even an almost physical tug that pulls you in a certain direction.

Signs you're a clairsentient:

- You 'feel' a lot of things, such as the rain coming, a person's attitude or when something doesn't feel right.

- Your friends think you are too sensitive and overreact to situations.

- You catch the emotions of other people around you and start to feel for them as well.

- You need to get away from social situations for a while to recharge your batteries. Being with people can be very overwhelming sometimes.

Claircognizance

This one is the hardest to explain because it doesn't make use of any faculty at all. While clairvoyance employs the intuitive vision, clairaudience intuitive hearing, clairalience intuitive smell and clairsentience intuitive feeling, there is no way claircognizance, or clearly knowing, gathers its information. It is like an important piece of knowledge has been automatically downloaded into your brain without any reason why. A claircognizant person just knows, without knowing why or how. He will be stumped when asked the question "Why?" because he cannot explain how he came about with the information he now has. Claircognizance is also not as dramatic as the other intuition sources because it doesn't come as a voice or a sudden movie in your mind. It simply appears inside your head from out of nowhere, quiet and unassuming yet very persistent at getting noticed. Faith is needed for you to realize that you are a claircognizant because there is no proof of intuition, except for the unquestionable 'knowing' that you feel deep inside.

Signs you're a claircognizant:

- You like to analyze and solve problems.

- Your best ideas seem to pop up from out of nowhere.

- You often finish other people's sentences for them because you know how they will end.

- You know when someone is lying to you.

- You know that things are going to happen or

that things are happening at the moment you think about them.

Access Meditations and Other Resources at this website: http://www.AngelicoBooks.com/Intuition

TRAINING YOUR INTUITION

Trust yourself. You know more than you think you do. —
Dr. Benjamin Spock

Here are a variety of steps and specific techniques that will allow you to clear the communication channels so that your intuition can reach out to you more easily. You don't need to do everything as stated in the next several chapters, but when you choose to follow one of the suggestions, you have to be willing to commit to it every time you do it. Not everything pointed out here will be easy. I don't mean that you will be struggling to become intuitive. On the contrary, I mean you will have to stop struggling for control of your mind and just let things go. Now *that* is definitely one of the hardest things to do. Also, you must maintain the intention to follow the plan you develop. Are you ready?

First let's start with some ideas that will make your life easier overall and improve your ability to communicate with your intuition. These probably won't be new, but if you are looking for another good reason to do them they will help you connect with your intuitive voice!

Create a good environment for the mind

The mind absorbs whatever it picks up, even when you're not paying attention to it. You know that cheesy song that is playing in the background while you work away on your computer? The mind picks it up and absorbs it and will amazingly provide you the answers when you find yourself in a situation where you need to know the lyrics. That's why you are sometimes surprised at yourself when you start singing a song with lyrics you didn't realize you knew. It works both ways, of course. It picks up good things, like cheesy song lyrics, and picks up bad things. Does this mean it is probably a bad idea to watch violent movies with bloody, gory scenes all the time? Yes, it does.

When the mind is muddled with unhealthy, disturbing thoughts, your intuition cannot find its way to you. It is essential that you control what messages are coming to you from your outside environment and filter out thoughts that are negative and unhelpful. You are certainly not the product only of the environment, for there is still a central part of you that remains *you*, but whatever you sense from the outside has an impact on what you are on the inside. The following can help you bring about an environment where the intuitive mind can flourish:

- **Take care of your body.** It's simple. A healthy body is a good home for a healthy mind. You probably already know how you can do this, but where work involves having to sit in front of the computer all day and play is sitting even longer in front of the TV the entire weekend, everybody needs a little reminding every now and then. Get your-self off your chair and exercise. Walk a little, move a little, and eat lots of healthy food to replace that processed food you get at McDonald's.

- **Clean up your home and beautify it.** Wouldn't it feel great if you could just get rid of the boxes of unused clothing you con-tinue to keep in plastic storage boxes under your bed? Keeping a lot of things that are no longer useful can weigh you down. One extra box that takes up space in your bedroom also occupies subconscious thought inside your mind. Free up that space. Get rid of your clut-ter. Set up a garage sale or donate it to the Salvation Army. Once it's all cleared up, open your windows and let some light in, rearrange your furniture to let all the old energy out and place some plants in strategic places to invite good energy in. Of course, these are only suggestions. De-cluttering is absolutely recommended, but you don't need to do a major house makeover if you don't want to.

- **Meditate.** You don't need to shave your head, don special robes and trek to the top of a mountain to meditate. You can simply do it in the quiet of your own bedroom. Meditation is an age-old spiritual practice done by the Buddhist monks for ages, but it's only recently that science has been catching up with it, only just now finding out the numerous benefits meditation poses for the mind, including developing intuition. Meditation will be discussed in further detail later in this book.

- **Be grateful.** Research by Robert Emmons, Ph.D. of the University of California at Davis and known as the leading gratitude researcher suggests gratitude is the one 'forgotten factor' in the equation for happiness. So how do you become grateful? It helps to get a sense of perspective. Think of the things that you have in your life that you love, and that perhaps other people don't have. I usually think about gratitude first thing in the morning and often start with being grateful for my warm bed and comfortable sheets.

- **Practice gratitude.** Every night, before you go to sleep, write down five to ten things that you are grateful for. Feel free to repeat them. This practice will start to give you an incentive to really look at your day and notice all the wonderful things around you.

- **Let go of negativity.** The easiest way for you to miss so much of what your intuition is telling you is to keep holding on to the negative thoughts that you harbor inside your head. The easiest way to finally let go of all the bottled-up negativity inside you is simply to consciously will yourself to do so. Tell yourself that you no longer need all these negative beliefs and memories and you are letting them go.

Similarly, steer clear of other sources of negativity that can mar your thoughts. All that bad news reported in the newspapers and on TV is not good for the mind. If something happens that is truly worth knowing about, it will find its way to you. Stay away from toxic people who prey on other people's energies and instill destructive thoughts. Instead, watch shows that make you laugh, switch to National Geographic and surround yourself with happy and positive people.

Building Your Intuitive Skills

Doesn't it seem counterproductive to train your intuition? After all, if it comes when you least expect it to, shouldn't you just sit there and wait until it decides to show itself to you? Training your intuition is not the same as forcing your intuition. It is more like training yourself to recognize when intuition comes to you. Once, at a seminar for young adult entrepreneurs, one of the participants asked, "When does intuition come to us?" The speaker, without even thinking about it, answered, "When does it *never* come to us?".

So, you see, the subconscious mind is continuously speaking to us in more ways than one, whether you recognize it or not. The goal of training is to allow you to realize when it is speaking to you and what it says. You can start by letting go of the need to control every single thing. Though it sounds simple enough it is not as easy as it seems, at least, at first.

To start training your intuition, you need to have a plan, just like the best athletes who religiously follow a rigorous workout plan and practice schedule to keep themselves in top shape. It doesn't have to be elaborate, but it has to have practical, objective and quantifiable steps so that you can come back to it later and measure your progress. Your subconscious mind will let you use clear and logical methods it normally doesn't understand, just so you can finally come to terms with it.

Here's the plan. Note that you don't have to follow every single suggestion. Just pick out the ones that you feel are working best for you and incorporate your own improvements to make this easier for you.

Intuitive Training Plan

1. Laying the groundwork – meditation and journaling

2. Specific Intuitive Exercises

- Intuition Connection Meditation
- Head, Heart, Gut
- Coin Flip
- Blind Reading
- Intuition Games

Meditate and be aware

More on Meditation. I wrote an entire book on meditation for busy people – you can find it at http://www.amazon.com/Beginning-Meditation-Busy-People-ebook/dp/B007MFLOWY/ref=sr_1_sc_1.

Why meditate?

Meditation is the quickest, easiest way to calm your mind so you can truly receive the communication from your intuition. The practice of meditation allows you to create your own space where your intuition can manifest itself without the disturbance of outside noise.

Unfortunately, the main reason why people don't meditate is also the main reason why they need to meditate. They are too overwhelmed by the busyness of their fast-paced lives. Have you ever tried to take a break from your numerous activities simply to sit down and rest, only to have your thoughts nag you about the countless other things that still need to be done? It's a vicious circle that gets in the way of you feeling at peace. If you plan to meditate, then do it and stick to it. Don't feel bad about not getting it right your first few tries. Meditation is not about doing it perfectly; it is about doing it now.

You also don't need sky-high goals to start a meditation practice. In a way, it is just like exercising your physical body. You don't aim for six-pack abs in a month or in two months or even in three months. You go for a more realistic goal of losing one pound each week. With meditation, you don't even need to set specific, measurable goals, except to set aside a few minutes every day for your practice.

Ideally you'd meditate for 40 minutes a day in the morning or evening. Few people I know can make the time for that length of meditation. If you can, research shows that even 10 minutes a day can help.

It's okay if you cannot find that amount of time to dedicate to meditation. But you can work in short moments of your day when you're doing things that don't really need conscious processing, such as folding the laundry or waiting in line. Use those moments as opportunities for meditating. Even two to three minutes every day can help.

Here are some simple instructions on meditation.

Begin by finding a safe and quiet place where you will not be disturbed for a few minutes. Sit in a relaxing position, with your back straight, feet flat on the floor and your hands folded loosely across your lap. Some people find that lying down is more comfortable for them, but that can sometimes lead you to sleep. Now relax. Relax your entire body starting with your toes. Let the relaxation move from your toes to your ankles, calves and on up, like a warm comfortable wave of energy spreading upwards until it relaxes the topmost part of your head.

Now become aware of your breath. Focus on each single inhalation and each exhalation as it easily comes and goes. Allow it to be slow or fast, however it is in the moment. Notice how cool the air is as you inhale. Now notice the warm air passing through your nostrils as you exhale. If thoughts arise, simply notice them and allow them to drift away. Just let them come and go, as though they are clouds passing across the sky. Simply gently steer your focus again to your breath.

Do you notice the expansive feeling of peacefulness that comes after a few minutes of meditation? It is within this sense of peace and calm that intuition is clearly sensed and accurately interpreted. Continue with your daily practice of meditation and you can easily guide yourself to go into a meditative state and access your intuition.

I have included a guided meditation file that you can download and save to your audio player. Simply put on your headphones and listen as you begin your meditation. This meditation will help you relax and raise your awareness so you can call forth your intuition from the depths of your subconscious mind.

If you're driving or working with machines, please don't listen to the file. Audio meditations are very relaxing and can sometimes even put you to sleep. You can download your guided meditation here at http://www.happyandhealthylives.com/intuition-meditations/

Journaling

A journal can also be an excellent tool to empty out your mind and allow your intuition to start to communicate with you. It can also help you start to notice the differences between your true intuition and random thoughts, emotions, and desires.

Keeping a journal to write your thoughts, feelings, emotions, fears, desires, dreams and whatever else that is going on inside you is an excellent way clear your mind and to start to notice your life and your intuitions. Looking back and reading the things you have written in your journal can really give you a sense of what is going on and recognize patterns in your thoughts and emotions that can help you eliminate the negatives and enhance the positives.

You can choose to write in a large, hard-bound notebook or a small, soft-cover that you can carry around with you wherever you go. If you are the type of person who gets inspired by the creaminess of the empty pages in fancy, leather-bound journals, by all means, fill them up with ink. Or if you prefer to write in separate pieces of index cards and keep them in a shoe box as your journal, you can do as you wish.

There is also online journaling software that you can access free or for a fee, and you can use this software to record your thoughts and anything else that might come up. The advantage of using software is that it is easier to organize your entries when they are uploaded online. The better programs even have features like mood-tracking to see how well you've been progressing emotionally in the past several months. The thing about journaling software, however, is that some people find its lack of intimacy off-putting. They find that the dog-eared notebook with creased pages is a better listener of their thoughts than their PCs or Macs. I find both work for me, so it really depends on you and your preferences.

Now, it's time to get down to writing. When you begin, dedicate a clear time and venue for journal writing. The reason why many people miss journaling for a few days, which eventually snowballs into an entire year, is because they don't set a specific time and place for writing. It's easy to promise to start a journaling habit and then forget about it one time, then another time, then another, until you go on forgetting about it until the next New Year's Eve for making another resolution. A good time to write is at night before you go to bed so that you can look back at the day's happenings and reflect on your thoughts about them. Writing in the morning before everyone else in the house wakes up is also a good idea because it helps you to plan your goals for the day and set the right mindset for achieving these daily goals.

Now comes the most challenging part of journal writing – the writing itself! What do you write about? The short answer is you can write about anything you want. If you're not satisfied with the short answer, I have no long answer, but I have several suggestions that you can start with.

You can use an intuition journal for a few different things:

1. Clearing your mind
2. Tracking your intuition
3. Asking questions of your intuition

Clearing Your Mind

A journal is an excellent tool to clear your mind. One exercise that really prepares me to listen to my intuitive self is called: Emptying Out.

In this exercise you set a timer for 5–10 minutes. You start by writing out everything that is in your head. This could be your to-do list, how you are feeling right now, any thoughts you have wandering through your brain. Just notice what comes up and keep writing. Write until the timer goes off. You might be surprised at what comes up.

Another exercise is to write about whatever you are curious about, what you'd like input from your intuition about.

Sometimes it's fun to start to write with your non-dominant hand (for me my left hand) and see what wisdom comes from that.

Generally though, clearing your mind is about opening up and letting whatever is in your head come out on paper so that you can see it clearly and make space for the quieter voice of your intuition.

Tracking Your' Intuition

Building your intuitive skills can be like bodybuilding, or learning chemistry. There are two parts to it: taking action, and recording your results.

You can certainly take action without recording your results, and still have fun and get in touch with your intuitive skills. But if you truly want to build an amazing connection with your intuition and learn to trust it in your daily life, recording your results will help. Give it shot!

Here's a basic outline of how it works.

1. Notice all the things that you think might be messages from your intuition. They may be things you see, hear, smell, feel, or just know. Every time you notice one, write it down. If you can do it with a curious, open mind, that helps it work most effectively. Jot it down in a

little notebook. I carry one in my purse. You might also write down which sense you get it through (see the later discussion on sense receptors). Was it a vision, a voice, a feeling, a scent, a knowing? Just jot it down in the spirit of scientific investigation. You might also jot down whether you chose to act on it or not.

2. About a week later, go back through your journal and see what you learn from it. You might learn that when you get visions, they are spot on, but voices are not. I was in an Intuitive Stock Picking group for awhile, and I learned that when I made decisions by seeing the price changes in a stock I was invariably wrong. In fact I was almost 100% wrong. But when I used my gut sense I was much better!

My point is that it's important to write down what you notice, and how you interpret it. Then later on go back and look at what actually happened with some curiosity and a scientific mind and see what you can learn about how your intuition communicates with you.

Formulating Questions

A great way to engage your intuition is directly – by asking questions. Journaling can help you create good questions and keep them in mind while you notice the different ways that your intuition gives you an answer.

What might you ask in your journal?

Ask specific questions of your intuition and see what answers you get. Often times I'll ask questions right before I go to sleep. Generally these are not 'yes' or 'no' questions. Any type of question will work to focus your intuition. I personally tend toward 'how to' questions. For example:

"How can I find a job that I love?"

"How do I know if this is the right relationship for me?"

Be sure to write questions in your journal and think about them so your intuition knows that you are seeking an answer. Then wait for a communication from your subconscious, being open to any type of answer.

How long should you write in your journal?

Make a daily practice of writing in your journal for at least 10 minutes. Write down what you noticed that day. What you noticed when interacting with people, any odd experiences or synchronicities.

Every week look back on the past week and start to put together any patterns.

Do you find that your inner voice tells you information clearly, but your inner vision tends to be wishful thinking? As you start getting a sense of how your intuition communicates with you, you'll start to trust it more and more and soon you'll have a trusted information source.

Practicing intuition techniques

In reality, if you create a good environment for your mind, meditate and write in your journal regularly, make decisions with your three intuition checks (Head, Heart and Gut – an explanation of these follow) and pursue a system to help you recognize your intuition, you hardly need other techniques to access your intuition. Simply freeing up the space in your mind that is usually reserved for unhelpful negativities can be enough for your intuition to come out loud and clear. Nonetheless, the following techniques are very useful for practicing and strengthening your intuition.

Check in with your head, heart and gut

Leadership experts David Dotlich, Peter Cairo and Stephen Rhinesmith wrote a book titled *Head, Heart, Gut: How the World's Best Companies Develop Leaders*. In their book, they explained how the best executives make decisions: by combining intellectual (head), emotional (heart) and intuitive (gut) factors related to a situation. For these three authors, a well-rounded leader knows how to devise business strategies, nurture relationships with his people and take risks all at the same time. The head, heart and gut are the three intuition checks and they have to be in agreement with one another for leaders to make the right decision.

You can apply this theory into your own personal decisionmaking. A lot of people are predominantly intellectual or emotional, which leads to choices that are, well, sometimes right and sometimes wrong. Intellectuals can sometimes make beneficial decisions with the help of the other two intuition checks, such as when you decide to exercise more because you know it's good for you. The head alone isn't always right, though. Your biggest problem when you decide only with your head is that you don't create meaningful relationships with the people and opportunities around you, and you don't experience things at a deeper, more profound, perspective.

On the other hand, people who make decisions based solely on their emotions almost always find themselves in emotional trouble when they real-ize they have been ignoring the signs the intellect was pushing their way. Don't get me wrong! You can make awesome heart-based decisions, such as when you excitedly say, "I can't wait to reach my goal of earning $5,000 a month!" There are times, however, when your dreams and emotions just keep you running around in circles, such as when you constantly find yourself broken-hearted because of romantic relationships that didn't work out.

The gut is normally where your subconscious mind sends its messages. However, what you *think* the gut tells you isn't always right. Think about the last time you went out on a limb and felt butterflies in your stomach. Were they good butterflies or bad butterflies? As I have mentioned before, these subconscious signals are always open to your interpretation. If you don't learn to understand what your gut is telling you, you may end up regretting your decision afterwards.

The thing is you have to check in with all three decision centers before you make a decision. I'm not saying do a head-heart-gut check when you can't decide whether to takeout pizza or Chinese (although it can work just fine for that as well), but for the more important decisions in your life, such as a new relationship or a career change, meditate and find out what each of these three is telling you.

Here's how to do it. I've made a recording of this tool that you can download from my website. You can find it here at http://www.happyandhealthy-lives.com/intuition-meditations/

1. Consider a decision that you want to make, or a situation that you want more information about. Allow an image or a sound or a feeling to form in front of you that represents the situation. We'll call this the 'icon' because it represents the situation. For example, if you are asking about a new job, you might picture the new workplace.

2. Now take the icon (which represents the situation), and imagine it moving into your head. Really allow yourself to get your head around it. Now notice whether with this image in your head you feel a sense of expansiveness, or a sense of contraction. Notice whatever thoughts, feelings, images, or ideas come into your head and write them down.

3. Now move the situation icon away from you and see how you feel with it away from you.

4. Take the situation icon and move it into your heart, in that area about four inches below your throat. When you move the icon into this space, notice if you get a sense of expansion,

or contraction. Write down any thoughts, feelings or ideas that you notice.

5. Move it away again and notice how it feels when you move it away.

6. Finally, move it into your gut area, about two inches below your navel and notice if you feel a sense of expansion or contraction. Write down any sensations or thoughts you notice.

7. Remove the icon from your gut and thank it and let it drift away.

8. Now review your notes and see what kind of pattern emerges.

You can also do this type of exercise with specific questions, and an example of that is below.

Let's say you meet someone and you are feeling drawn to them as a romantic partner, as a business partner, or even as a friend. To check with your intuition about the relationship you can form an image of them in your mind. Bring that image into your head, right above your eyebrows. Notice what thoughts come up and how you feel. Now pull the picture out and put it in your heart. Notice how you feel now. Is it a good feeling? Excitement? Fear? Confusion? Is it an opening or a closing? Now pull the image out. Now allow the image of that person to float into your gut. How does that feel? Good? Uncomfortable?

You might notice that you get some insights about this person by checking in with these different centers. Listen to them!

Be sure to check out the recorded version of this meditation. You can find it at http://www.happyandhealthylives.com/intuition-meditations/

Every time you have a difficult time making a decision, you can listen to this meditation to help you tune in to your three intuition checks. If the answers don't come immediately, don't fret. It takes some time before these three can come into agreement with one another. When the right opportunity presents itself to you, the head, heart and gut automatically synchronize with one another to let you know you're doing the right thing.

Flip a coin

Can flipping a coin help you make better decisions? Certainly, but not in the way you think it will. If you have gone through the usual daily meditations and painstakingly stuck to your plan but still come up empty-handed, calling heads or tails may give you better insight than meditating.

Let's say you're torn between two job offers and you can't make up your mind about which offer to accept. Assign each job offer to each side of the coin. If the coin lands heads, you have to go with the job assigned to that side of the coin. If it lands tails, the decision is to accept that job. Now, notice how you feel when the coin lands. Are you happy with the outcome of your coin-flipping? Do you feel at peace with the choice that the coin made for you? What if you feel ill at ease with the result? The coin-flipping technique doesn't really tell you what to do. How random the world would be if we all made decisions by flipping coins! However, this technique can show you what your heart really wants by giving you insight into how you feel or what you think when the coin lands heads or tails.

Do a blind reading

When stuck in a trough, a blind reading can help you answer a question you've been having difficulty with. To do this, sit down and take two or more blank index cards and write down all the possible answers you are considering. Turn them over so that they are facing right-side down and shuffle the index cards until you no longer remember which one contains which answer. Then mentally ask your question and focus on each of the index cards one by one. How do you feel with each card? Which card draws you the most strongly? Which card repels you the most? Notice the feelings, thoughts and sensations that come up with each of these cards. The answer to your question just might be found in the card that makes you feel the most comfortable.

Play intuition games

Games that can strengthen your intuition are just that – games. Although you are playing with a goal – that is, to help yourself recognize and under-stand your intuition better – you probably won't get much out of it if you're playing to win. Don't focus too much or try too hard. The same guidelines in meditation apply in playing intuition games: 1. Relax. 2. Let go. 3. Be aware. Let's take a look at some of these games:

1. Children like to play the classic 'I'm Thinking of a Number' game. It goes like this. Your partner thinks of a number between a certain range of numbers, normally 1 to 10 for beginners and gradually widening its range as you get better, and you try to guess the number. You win when you guess the number correctly. Now, the difference with the children's classic is that your partner has to project the number to you. Have him think of the number in whatever way is most comfortable for him – pictures, words or feelings, so that you can try to 'catch on' these mental projections.

2. Another game you can play is the twist to another children's favorite – Hide and Seek. Normally, you hide and whoever is 'it' goes looking for you, but this time, have the person you are playing with choose an object and hide it in one part of the room. You have to

go out first, to ensure there is no peeking. When your friend has hidden the object, you can come back inside and search for it. The catch is that you don't do it manually; you do it intuitively. Find a comfortable place to sit down and relax and have the your friend send you thoughts of where he or she hid the object. Listen to whatever messages come to you and see if you can find the object. You can also play 'colder' / 'warmer', and if you guess one spot your partner can let you know if it is closer or further away than the previous spot.

Access Meditations and Other Resources at this website: http:www.AngelicoBooks.com/Intuition

WHEN NOT TO TRUST YOUR INTUITION

Intuition vs. Wishful Thinking

One of the biggest challenges people have in learning to trust their intuition is telling the difference between intuition and wishful thinking. Here's a quick rule of thumb.

If it feels calm, clear and centered it's probably intuition. If it feels forced, fearful, or based in desire, it may well be desire and it's best to double-check it.

Things That Can Cloud Your Intuition

One question that often comes up is: What is the difference between intuition and profiling? It's a fine line. Profiling is when a person makes a judgment about another person or situation based on a prejudice perhaps race, gender, clothing or mannerisms. Intuition is a deeper communication. Part of the journey of learning to use your intuition effectively is to notice the difference for yourself. We all have prejudices, and when we look at them and accept them and choose not to act on them, we can learn to trust our intuitive sense of a situation despite our prejudice.

Some other factors that can cloud our intuition include:

- *emotional bias* – if we have a strong emotional stake in the answer we might not get a clear reading

- *using only intuition* – not considering the 'facts'

- *stress* – some intuition is received best in stressful situations, and some intuition needs a quiet mind

- *context* – we may have great intuitive insights in some parts of our lives and not in others.

As you start to record your intuitions and test their accuracy, you'll start to hone your own abilities to know the difference between real intuition and a false reading.

When to go with your gut and when not to

"Your time is limited, so don't waste it living someone else's life. Don't be trapped by dogma which is living with the results of other people's thinking. Don't let the noise of others' opinions drown out your own inner voice. And most important, have the courage to follow your heart and intuition." – Steve Jobs

The world isn't black and white. There are a lot of gray areas that even the subconscious mind sometimes has trouble understanding. Yes, there are times when going with what your gut tells you is the only acceptable thing to do, and there are also times when it is most likely not your gut talking to you but something else. This is when you have to take over and consciously decide whether to listen or to ignore.

How do you distinguish between the two? To put it simply, you are listening to your gut when you feel relaxed and comfortable and even happy and satisfied. When you feel pressure or the need to take control, it is not your intuition talking to you but your fears.

Listen: When you're playing to win. There's really not much time to over-analyze each and every single move you make on the sports field. The sub-conscious mind recognizes this and swiftly takes over, telling you which way your body should go to land the best moves that lead to a win. Surprisingly, intuition also takes over in chess players who play blitz chess, a five-minute version of the original game which normally requires massive logical and analytical thinking skills.

Ignore: When investing your money. The value of money is subject to the fluctuations of external forces that we generally aren't aware of until they are already there. Resist the temptation to invest your money in any deal that doesn't sound profitable because, more often than not, it isn't. An example is the rapid rise and fall of the dot-com companies at the start of the millennium, when investors made a mad dash at the stock exchange for the dot-coms because, well, something told them dot-coms will constitute the new economy, even though most of them had negative earnings at the end of each quarter. Dot-coms may be profitable now but the bubble still burst and they lost their investments in the early 2000s.

Listen: When you need a second opinion. Nobody, not even the best physician in the entire world, knows your body more than you do. The problem with some doctors is that they tend to rely too heavily on standardized medical tests and dismiss what their patients are telling them about what they feel. If you feel that your doctor's diagnosis was incomplete or incorrect, follow your hunch and talk to another physician for a second opinion, or even a third! You definitely shouldn't be taking chances when it comes to your health.

Ignore: When you want to quit your job. Going through your list of pros and cons instead of following your gut-feel can help you make the decision. Leaving your job, especially if you still don't have another job to go to or if the next job you plan to take is going to be just as problematic as the present one, is a decision that has to be made largely by the intellect.

Listen: When you're making a moral decision. The first thing that comes to mind when you learn that your best friend's boyfriend is cheating on her is usually the right thing to do. However, it is important that you also weigh the consequences of any actions that you are planning to take because there are other people's feelings and relationships that are at stake. In this case, it is better to use the head-heart-gut check before taking rash action.

Ignore: When hiring someone. A candidate's pleasant personality does help him win the job, but it still isn't as important as the ability to do the job and to do the job well. Besides, any first impressions that you make of a person are based on a number of factors, such as his resemblance to your best friend or that he is wearing your favorite scent, that are usually not crucial to his performance of the job.

Listen: When you're making a big purchase. Research shows that people are happier with their big-ticket purchases when they spent less time thinking the purchase over. So, for example, if you're on the lookout for a new home and you find one that feels absolutely right for you, then it most likely is.

Ignore: When judging the sincerity of people. Do you know that even with tons of information being published on how people can easily detect liars through their body language, most of us still fail at deciphering the truth or lies behind a person's statement? The best we have is nothing more than a 50–50 chance of pointing out the liars from the good guys. Pretty dismal, if you think about it. The best way to discern whether a person is telling the truth or is pulling your leg is to look into his past behavior. Of course, people can change and it's unfair to judge others completely on past mistakes, but trusting others has to be based on a clean record of sincerity.

You can access Meditations and Other Resources at this website: http://www.AngelicoBooks.com/Intuition

PUTTING IT ALL TOGETHER

Learn your style

Earlier, when we discussed the different sources of intuition, were you able to identify yourself as being dominant in at least one of the intuitive senses? Do you know whether you are clairvoyant, clairaudient, clairsentient or claircognizant? Or are you a combination of the five?

It's important to know how you tune in because this will help you to determine the fastest and easiest way to get to your goal. It is like when you want to reach a destination and you choose between walking flying, bicycling, or rowing a boat to get there. Which one of these modes of transportation will help you arrive at your destination in the clearest way possible?

Your intuitive style is probably similar to your learning style. If you're having a difficult time deciphering how your subconscious mind speaks to you, take a look at how you consciously try to receive and process information. Do you learn best by using charts, diagrams or maps, or by having someone explain something to you? Perhaps you like to be left alone and rely on hands-on experience to learn or you simply like to mull things over in your head.

When you notice something, feel it. Allow it to make itself fully present to your conscious mind, again without forcing it to be anything else. Let your intuition come to you by consciously asking it to do so. Relax into a deep and meditative state where you can connect more easily with your subconscious and talk to it. Think these words to yourself: "I now allow my subconscious to tell me things that are beneficial for me." Then, sit quietly and meditate to allow your subconscious mind to fill in the space with the inner knowledge that *you are opening up for it.*

Ask questions and listen for answers

Be proactive. Yes, listen for your intuitive voice and ask questions. Your intuition is your partner. It has all sorts of information that can make your life easier. So ask.

You can ask questions all the way from "What should I do with my life?" to "Should I go to the party on Saturday?" Your intuition is not picky about answering. Then wait for an answer and notice how you get your answers. Write down the question and every day see what kinds of answers you get when reflecting on it.

Record your intuition

Keeping a log of your intuitive encounters allows you to come back to them later and check on them. Your journal is the excellent place to jot down any sudden thoughts, hunches or nudges from within.

Don't try to limit yourself to your dominant intuitive style, though. Your intuition is very patient and will find all the ways it can to reach you.

If you ignore your hunches because you mistake them for biased conclusions, your mind will start to make you notice other things, such as the coincidences around you... because coincidences are not merely chance occurrences of unrelated events pretending to be related. For other people, a coincidence may be just that... a coincidence. For you, it may be a synchronicity, your mind's way of telling you something that you shouldn't pass up.

And, if you still dismiss these synchronicities, your mind will speak to you in a more obvious but still very symbolic manner: your dreams. These, along with the little nagging thoughts, feelings, and tugs in your stomach, the sudden reappearance of things you thought were lost, and everything else you can't provide an explanation for, but you feel as though need to be heeded, should all be written down.

Come back to it

The last and most important part of the plan is to come back to your record and check if your intuitions were true. If so, your interpretations are reliable and it would be beneficial to continue practicing the use of your intuition.

But what if your intuitions were incorrect? Does it mean they were unreliable? One of the things I have learned is that your intuition is never wrong, but that you may mistake it for something else. It happens because we still use logic to try to interpret these intuitions and logic can still get us wrong.

To be able to trust, accept and understand your intuition demands nothing from you, yet you have to let go of a lot of the things most people have doggedly held on to most of their lives. The belief that the only right way to see things is from the rational, logical perspective; the compulsion to hold fast to material things we own only because the Jones have it; and the false sense of urgency a fast-paced life controlled by a motley of interests that profit from your being so busy – these are the three things you need to give up for you to freely come to your intuition.

Your intuition is a very, very powerful thing. Once you learn to harness the power that it brings, the power to change your life and the lives of others is now in your hands. Use it for the good of all.

Access Meditations and Other Resources at this website: http://www. AngelicoBooks.com/Intuition

APPENDIX:
FAMOUS EXAMPLES OF
INTUITION

Abraham Lincoln. Three days before his assassination, Abraham Lincoln related to his friends a dream that had kept annoying him since he had it. Ward Hill Lamon, one of his friends and bodyguards, was there to hear the President talk about his dream and recorded what he said, to be published later in his book *Recollections of Abraham Lincoln*. In his dream, the President was lying on his bed when he heard muffled sobs coming from the East Room. He sat up and began to follow the sound of weeping, seeing the lights on in every room he passed, still hearing the sounds of weeping, but he could see no mourners. As he approached the East Room, Lincoln saw a throng of soldiers guarding a coffin and mourners all around. When he demanded to know who was dead inside the White House, one of the soldiers answered, "The President. He was killed by an assassin."

Samuel L. Clemens (more popularly known as Mark Twain). America's greatest humorist had an interest in 'strange things', as was exhibited in some of his works. Mark Twain was born in 1835, just two weeks after Halley's Comet, which only comes in close contact with our home planet every 75 to 76 years, brushed past the Earth. A year before Mark Twain passed away, he was reported to have said, "I came in with Halley's Comet in 1835. It is coming again next year, and I expect to go out with it. It will be the greatest disappointment of my life if I don't go out with Halley's Comet." Sure enough, his death was not a disappointment for, on April 10 1910, just one day after Halley's Comet once again passed by, he died at 6:30 in the evening.

Mrs. Constance Gracie. Ian Stevenson, an investigator of paranormal events wanted to know exactly how many instances had intuition and premonition taken over during the disaster of the Titanic. Around 50 had been claimed, but after stringent evaluations, Stevenson had whittled it down to 19 cases. One of the most famous of these instances is Colonel Archibald Gracie's silent plea to send through the spiritual network to his family the news of how he died. Colonel Gracie was treading feebly in the freezing Atlantic waters after the lifeboat he and his friends were on turned over. He thought he was going to die in a few moments and so he "prayed that my spirit could go to them and say, 'Good-bye, until we meet again in heaven'." At that moment, Mrs. Constance Gracie was tossing and turning between the sheets in her sister's house in New York, not knowing why sleep wouldn't come to her as it normally did. Then came the tiny voice inside her head, "On your knees and pray". Mrs. Gracie turned her prayer book to a random page and prayed "For those at sea". Colonel Archibald Gracie was able to cling to the top of the overturned lifeboat and survived to tell the tale.

Winston Churchill. The admirable statesman himself admitted that he always felt as though he had something that was there to protect him. When he escaped from his captors in South Africa during the Boer War, he was unable to get on a freight train that would take him over the enemy lines. His only hope was to find a native Kaffir who was friendly to the British and would not hand him over to the authorities. For some reason, Winston Churchill was drawn to a particular house in a Kaffir kraal. He knocked on the door and asked for help and learned that it was the only British-friendly house within a 20-mile radius.

Joan of Arc. When Saint Joan of Arc was tried for heresy, the inquisitor told her that it was only her imagination when she said that God speaks to her. In answer to this, Joan said, "How else would God speak to me, if not through my imagination?". At around the same time English troops burned the town of Domremy, she began hearing voices inside her head whom she later identified as Saint Michael, Saint Catherine and Saint Margaret. Initially, she was terrified of these voices, which only grew clear to her whenever she was away from other people. She had gradually come to accept them and listen to what they were saying, even claiming that she could summon them at will. It was these voices that instructed Joan to help the Dauphin and go to Orleans and drive the English away.

My story (not so famous). I used to be strident in my opposition to all this "hocus pocus". I was probably one of the most 'out-of-touch' people around. My background in the hard sciences taught me that if it can't be proven with a double-blind study by researchers around the world, then it's not true.

I had a lucrative job in corporate America and was dutifully climbing the corporate ladder. I was well on my way to the BMW and the corner office, and that was my goal. Then I got a very strong hunch that I should leave my job. I thought it was completely ridiculous. So I ignored it. A few days later I got a physical pain in my body, and a sense that I should leave.

I mentioned it to a friend, and she suggested that I check it out and worked with me to explore my options – just in case. That small still voice was insistent. It kept telling me I'd be happier in the long run to let go of this job. Go ahead, it said, I assure you it'll turn out perfectly.

So, after also thinking it through and making a plan, I gave up my lucrative corporate job and started exploring something that had always been a dream of what I might do when I retired. I became a coach and writer.

About a week after I quit my job, my division was sold and many painful (I heard from ex-co-workers) months later the division was disbanded.

Honestly, this didn't convince me about intuition, but it did get me to start considering it, and the more I learned about the science of intuition, the more convinced I became. Now, many books, seminars and journals later I am coaching my clients on how to improve their communication with their intuition!

That was the start of a long, fruitful and very happy friendship between my intuitive self and my mind. Since then, I've come to depend on it for some of my toughest decisions.

The results in my life have been spectacular. For starters, I'm more focused when working with tight deadlines. I'm worried less about the decisions; I'm concentrating more on getting the task at hand completed.

Since I'm under less pressure and feel less stress, I find that I'm more creative – both at work and at home. I've taken part in creative activities I haven't enjoyed in years.

Even my friends have noticed a change in me. I eventually told them what I've been doing, listening to that small voice cajoling me. Some of them said it took me long enough to listen! Others, though, wanted to know how I developed it. So I explained it to them step by step. They too began to experience benefits.

They encouraged me to record my intuition-building program, to write about it in enough detail that others like yourself could benefit from it. At first I resisted. But, ironically (or perhaps it really wasn't!) my intuition told me to put all my secrets to boosting your intuitive thought into an easy-to-follow system. How could I refuse?

This book is the result of my friends' suggestions and, most importantly, the urging of my intuition. And I am truly grateful to them all. The goal is for you to develop your own intuition or hone the voice inside you that calls out to you.

The exercises in this book have been used by myself, close friends and others. They will help you develop your intuition and in doing so you too can gain peace of mind, reach goals you never thought were possible and enjoy life to its fullest.

www.ingramcontent.com/pod-product-compliance
Lightning Source LLC
Chambersburg PA
CBHW061155040426

42445CB00013B/1696